SCOTTISH MASTERS

The National Galleries of Scotland, in its three buildings, the Portrait Gallery, the National Gallery and the Gallery of Modern Art, holds the nation's collection of Scottish art. It is a marvellously rich and varied collection ranging in date from the 16th century to the present day, including works by artists of world stature and by others hardly known outside the Galleries themselves.

SCOTTISH MASTERS is a new series designed to make some of the most interesting and delightful Scottish artists more widely known. In 1984 the Patrons of the National Galleries of Scotland was founded under the Presidency of HRH The Duke of Edinburgh to channel extra financial assistance from the private sector to the National Galleries. They are enormously grateful to the Scottish Post Office Board for the generous sponsorship of this series. This has enabled these attractively designed monographs to be published at such a reasonable price. How appropriate that the masters of communications themselves should help us to communicate to Scotland, and beyond, the heritage of us all.

Explanation is an essential part of the Galleries' purpose: so also is acquisition. We are doubly grateful to the Scottish Post Office Board for the generous financial help they have given us to boost our active policy of purchasing the finest works of Scottish art for our national collections. We are delighted that the Board share our view that for a lively gallery acquisition and explanation must go hand in hand.

The Scottish Post Office Board's imaginative support of the National Galleries is just one part of their enlightened programme of involvement with both the visual and performing arts, reminding us of the central role that the Post Office plays in Scottish life.

THE VISCOUNT WEIR,
Chairman of the Patrons of the National Galleries of Scotland.

ROBERT BEGG Esq, CBE,
Chairman of the Trustees of the National Galleries of Scotland.

Alexander Carse (c. 1770–1843) Self Portrait.
Scottish National Portrait Gallery.

A l e x a n d e r
C A R S E
c . 1 7 7 0 - 1 8 4 3

BY LINDSAY ERRINGTON

AN OUTLINE OF CARSE'S LIFE

Had Alexander Carse been born in 17th century Holland he might now rejoice in a title such as "The little master of the ale-house brawls" or "the master of the country relations". As it is, he has merely received the affectionate but uninformative nickname of "Old" Carse—presumably given to distinguish him from his less able son William.

The facts about his early life are scanty. It is said that he was a native of East Lothian and that he was initially trained as a stay-maker but his date of birth is unknown—though one may guess it took place in the 1770s. At some point he worked as a pupil and assistant to David Allan, who died in 1796, and whose idiosyncratic outlook on life is stamped on Carse's earliest imaginative drawings. The views of *Leith Races* and of *Oldhamstocks Fair* (fig 1) might pardonably be confused with drawings by Allan. The main body of Carse's earliest work however seems to have consisted of topographical views of country houses, and Hopton (sic) House, Newbattle House, Barn Bougle (sic) Castle, Bellevue, and Preston Hall were engraved by Robert Scott in 1795 and 6 after drawings by Carse. Other views showed Hermitage of Braid, Dunbar Castle ruins, and Edinburgh with

Fig 1
OLDHAMSTOCKS FAIR.

Holyrood and the Castle. This drudgery, as it may well have seemed, was interspersed with figurative subjects for book illustrations, and volumes of *The Life of Robinson Crusoe* (1795) and of Burns' poems (1802) appeared embellished with plates after Carse. The four illustrations to Burns, *The Holy Fair, The Cottar's Saturday Night, Tam O'Shanter* and *The Jolly Beggars* show that by 1802 Carse's feet were already planted on the path he was to follow for the rest of his life.

He clearly possessed ambitions unsatisfied by the restricting genre of house portraiture, and on 16 December 1801 was admitted to the Trustees' Academy as a student. At the Academy he would have received a very basic training in drawing, but would have benefited from the compositional painting classes introduced by the master Graham. There was unfortunately then no life drawing available.

Carse's first known oil painting dates from 1803, and the opening in Edinburgh in 1808, of regular exhibitions for living artists, seems to have offered him an outlet for numerous small genre scenes painted in oils, rather than the gouache or watercolour he had hitherto employed.

From 1808 until 1815 Carse was a regular exhibitor with the Associated Artists, usually showing several pictures, and in 1812, a peak year, sending twelve. Criticisms in the *Scots Magazine* indicate that his works were well received. In 1809 he was praised for his *Wooer's Visit* "composed with great delicacy and judgement, well drawn and admirably coloured, somewhat in the style and manner

of Wilkie, our *Scots Teniers*". His *Chapman* of the previous year had been admired for its characterisation. "The self complacency and cajoling manner of the principal personage, are admirably depicted; and the effect produced on the bystanders is finely and characteristically pourtrayed (sic)". In 1812 the reviewer singled out the picture now generally regarded as Carse's masterpiece, *The Country Relations,* and recorded "The preference which this picture seems to obtain in the eye of the general observer, over all others exhibited by this artist . . . we recommend him to continue to pursue this department of art (ie familiar life) since it appears to be his forte."

At the height of his limited powers, and perhaps inspired with over-confidence by these or similar praises, and also by the example of his fellow countryman Wilkie's phenomenal success in the South, Carse departed for London in 1812, or at the beginning of the next year. He continued to send pictures to the Edinburgh exhibitions, but his main effort seems thereafter to have been directed towards pictures for the Royal Academy, at which he showed works from 1812 until 1820, and the British Institution, where he showed from 1813 until 1820. He was constantly changing his address, moving every year or two, from Stanhope Street to Vine Street, Piccadilly, from Vine Street to Prospect Row, Pentonville, from Prospect Row to 2 Grenville Street, Clarendon Square, and then from 2 to 7 Grenville Street. This restless shifting of quarters scarcely seems like a sign of prosperity, and, in 1820 Carse moved back to Edinburgh. The immediate cause may have been a circular letter from the Royal

Institution to "Artists in London" dated "Edin. 27th May 1820", a copy of which was sent to Carse, and from which he would have learnt of an exhibition to be held in Edinburgh in March 1821. Although the artists in London were promised free carriage of their pictures by waggon, Carse may have decided that his London experiment had not been entirely successful, that artistic prospects in Edinburgh were brightening, and that it was time to return home. From 1821 he ceased to exhibit in London, and confined his efforts first to the Royal Institution for the Encouragement of the Fine Arts (from 1821 to 1830) and then from 1827 until 1836 to the newly created Royal Scottish Academy.

Either because he may, whilst living in the South, have sent only second rate works to the Edinburgh exhibitions, or because the *Scots Magazine's* reviewer disliked his having abandoned Edinburgh, Carse received, in 1815, a savage attack in that magazine, instead of the usual benign commendation. "From the many opportunities of improvement this artist must have had since he went *to town,* we confess to have felt disappointment in viewing the works he has now exhibited. No. 34 'The witches late-wake' . . . is a very vulgar *bit* . . . No. 51 'The hot argument', is another instance of the coarseness of the mind of this unfortunate gentleman, who truly appears to us to have made lately no advancement whatever in art." The reviewer, who, a few years before had mildly mentioned that Carse appeared to have given insufficient attention to "studies after the antique", now multiplied his deficiencies to include "want of knowledge of figure drawing and perspective". In truth Carse's earlier lack of training was beginning to catch up with him as a new and more thoroughly educated generation of Scottish artists, with more sophisticated professional standards, began to emerge. Nevertheless his energies were not exhausted, and in 1822 he embarked on the largest, most elaborate, and most ambitious project of his life, *George IV Landing at Leith,*

Fig 2
GEORGE IV LANDING AT LEITH.

(fig 2)—5 feet high and 11 feet long, containing several hundred figures—many of them portraits—various military uniforms, ships, and a representation of the harbour and waterfront at Leith. Two other artists present in Edinburgh to record the ceremonies of the King's visit were of course Turner and Wilkie—Carse had placed himself in competition with exalted contenders.

During the next decade, though active as a painter, Carse fell into serious financial difficulties, to such a degree that he was compelled to apply for assistance to the Royal Institution's Trustees of the Spalding Fund for the relief of decayed and superannuated artists. His sad and touching letter of application deserves to be quoted in full for the light it throws on his career.

"I humbly beg leave to represent to you that I have for 40 years past been a painter, chiefly of domestic, familiar, and poetical subjects, and if I have not attained the distinction which I diligently sought for by assiduous study and practice, I may impute it to the want of means in my early life, and the want of those excellent models for improvement in Drawing, which happily for the rising Artists are now collected in the Academy of the Board of Trustees, and accessible to them all.

But under numerous disadvantages I have steadily and cheerfully employed my pencil upon those subjects which Fancy & Observtions on life and character, suggested to me: And without meaning to speak in my own praise, I may be allowed to say that my productions have frequently been honoured with the approbation of very competent Judges, and purchased by them.

I am now my Lords & Gentlemen considerably advanced in years; I have suffered much of late by ill health and I have a wife and nine children solely dependant on my health and success for their support.

If you are pleased to consider this simple statement of facts, and to regard my pictures with a favourable eye, I would fain flatter myself that you will be induced to confer upon me the honour and the benefit of admitting me as one of the associated Artists of your Institution. And as I have ever maintained an irreproachable character, I trust I may be found worthy of the great act of goodness which I take the liberty to solicit from you."

Carse's plea was supported by the signatures of nineteen Scottish artists amongst whom the most eminent were Thomas Duncan, Alexander Nasmyth, and William Allan. He obtained £25.00 from the Spalding Fund and was advised to try to obtain settlement with his creditors by a composition. His letters on this matter are simply headed "Abbey", which suggests that he had been forced to move to the only area in Edinburgh where he could safely escape arrest for debt. Evidently he continued to receive a yearly annuity from the Spalding Trustees until the end of his life. On Tuesday 21st February 1843 an order was made to pay him the annuity, and on the 2nd March 1843 his death is mentioned as making a vacancy in the Trust's annuitants. His death therefore, which was previously vaguely placed c1838 can now be fixed as having occurred in February 1843 only two years after that of Wilkie, his far more celebrated countryman, and initially his follower.

THE CHARACTER OF CARSE'S ART

Carse's career spans the chasm between the first naive attempts at Scottish genre by David Allan in the eighteenth century and the great upsurge of artistic activity amongst the new masses of home-bred, home-trained Scottish artists in the first half of the nineteenth. His art is a minor and in many ways a provincial one, but full nevertheless of interest and delight, for however hampered by an inadequate training, he possessed an original mind, and the good sense to confine himself to the kind of subject-matter he really understood. Had he been born half a century earlier he might never have risen from the rut of engraver's hack. Had he been born half a century later, his art school training would have given him skills equal to his intentions.

His early drawings have already been briefly mentioned in the outline of his life. Amongst these the view of Leith races is full of humorous incidents invented by the artist. On the left is a fiddler so drunk as to be unaware that his violen has been snatched from below the bow. In the centre the sweep's boy accidently brushes a lady's skirt. On the right the passengers are tipped out of a cart as the owner unhitches his

Fig 3
VIEW OF NEWHALL HOUSE
Engraving after Alexander Carse for the 1808 edition of
THE GENTLE SHEPHERD.

horse. *Oldhamstocks Fair,* in a similar style, seems particularly to have caught the attention of the young Wilkie, who adapted the idea for his own *Pitlessie Fair.* Interestingly enough, it may have been through the commission from Sir James Hall of Dunglass for the *Willow Cathedral* drawing that Carse also came to paint *Oldhamstocks Fair.* This little village, near the East Lothian coast, had been for centuries the location of a fair. In the *First Statistical Account* of the parish Sir James is recorded as the only resident heritor out of eight, and it is quite possible that he was sufficiently interested in local history to ask Carse to paint the fair for him. *Oldhamstocks* is dated 1796, and the *Willow Cathedral* may well belong to the same year.

Sir James Hall of Dunglass was not alone as a quirky scholar and landowner who found a use for Carse's skills to illustrate his theories. Robert Brown of Newhall, about whom little is known apart from his passionate conviction that his own estate had once been Allan Ramsay's model for the scenery of the poem *The Gentle Shepherd,* published a series of essays supporting this contention in *The Edinburgh Magazine* of 1801-1803. His thesis was illustrated by engravings of various locations commissioned by himself. One of these was after a drawing by Carse, and later on in 1808, when Brown's essays were published in two volumes, along with the text of Ramsays poem, as *The Gentle Shepherd with illustrations of the scenery,* Carse supplied two further illustrations (fig 3). The more elaborate of these two new plates showed Ramsay's returned Royalist, Sir William Worthy, gazing wistfully at "his" house,

semi-ruinous after his long exile. For this Carse had to reconstruct the supposed earlier appearance of Newhall House, and clothe Sir William in period costume. Other recorded work by Carse at Newhall no longer exists. It may partly have been from the company of eccentric patrons like Sir James Hall and Robert Brown that Carse derived his antiquarian concern with the past. Certainly some remarks made by Brown in his edition of *The Gentle Shepherd* are quite as applicable to Carse's later paintings of traditional football games, weddings and family prayers, as they are to the plates in Brown's book. "Mr Allan's aquatintas keep alive Ramsay's *Dramatis Personae,* with great fidelity in dress, character, and expression; and the accurate *Views* . . . now presented to the public precisely as they were seen, are intended to preserve and exhibit, in the plain unembellished garb of truth, their artless and genuine *places of residence* . . . and their value increases with the same rapidity as the characters, and country change, from culture; and the possibility of tracing out many of the resemblances diminishes, before they are irrecoverably lost." Almost, this might stand for Carse's motto in much of his later work.

The old and the traditional were not then, however, at the beginning of the nineteenth century, the only claims on his brush. His three little views of Midfield Cottage, Lasswade are rare, indeed unique records, for their date and place, of an actual fashionable cottage ornée and its occupants. Only a short distance from Edinburgh, and surrounded by strikingly pretty scenery, Lasswade formed a convenient rural retreat for persons of taste. According to Richard Emerson, Midfield Cottage (no longer standing) together with Barony House (which still exists) may both have been designed by Clerk of Eldin, who made drawings for a very similar cottage at about this time. Midfield, as the outside views indicate (fig 4 and 5), was originally a row of

Fig 4
GARDEN FRONT OF MIDFIELD COTTAGE,
1807.

genuine cottages tidied up and embellished. The trim shrubberies and curving borders outside, and the internal features which speak of modern comfort, elegance and artistic taste—the plaster statuary, the harp, the pictures, ornaments and fitted carpet, even the inmates in their white muslin dresses—are all as unlike the settings and furniture of a real cottage as anything could well be. The chief architectural feature, the bow window with its framed view towards Hillend on the Pentlands, set Carse an interesting challenge in lighting that he responded to with an inexperienced but appreciative eye.

Some years later, in *The Country Relations* of 1812, he exploited all his resources as an interior painter, deploying

to an entirely new purpose what he had learnt when recording the interior of the Lasswade cottage ornée. His delight in the complex effects of two shafts of light crossing at right angles to each other through the two windows, and outlining the necks and shoulders of the three elegant urban ladies, makes one wish that he had

Fig 5
ENTRANCE FRONT OF MIDFIELD COTTAGE,
1807.

attempted this kind of subject more often. His picture is a most unusual combination of sophistication of subject and vision but semi-naivety of technique. When compared with Wilkie's contemporary, and thematically similar picture, *The Letter of Introduction* which also confronts town with country, *The Country Relations* lags far behind in draughtsmanship and sheer elegance of execution, but rather surprisingly exhibit sensitivities towards light effects which are lacking in Wilkie at that date. There is reason to believe, from the placing of the windows and doors, that Carse's room is not a portrait of a possible place but a contrived stage set. If this is so, then his choice of precisely those articles of furniture, carpeting, and ornament that will most clearly explain the status and ambitions of his townees is a triumph of imaginative selection.

Carse's country visitors have doubtless come from a farmhouse with unplastered ceilings, stone flagged floors and rudimentary deal tables and chairs such as we see in plate 5. Despite their astonishment and embarrassment as, dressed in their homely shawls, they survey the splendid fitted carpet, modern polished chairs, pictures, musical instrument and even perhaps the parrot, Carse's rendering is not a satire in any way. A genuine feeling of warmth and good will prevails. The two men beam and grip each other's hands. It is the women who, separated by divergent fashions, find it harder to make contact with each other. There is unfortunately no evidence that

Carse ever tackled social comedy of this quality again.

The difference between the living standards of town and country shrank rapidly in the period following Carse's picture. The minister of Mid Calder for example was to recall, in 1839, how rural customs had changed since 1795. At one time both the farmer's family and the servants dipped their spoons in the same communal dish of porridge in a mud floored kitchen, and sat together "promiscuously" round the kitchen hearth, but gradually habits of urban gentility crept in, so that by 1839 the farmer would have had his own exclusive family parlour, with its carpeting, polished table, and porcelain service. The contrast of manners which Carse records was thus in itself a fragile thing on the way

Fig 6
CHRIST'S KIRK ON THE GREEN.

Fig 7
THE DOONIES VERSUS THE CROONIES ON
NEW YEARS DAY.

out, as were perhaps the other games and pastimes he depicts. Certainly John Sommers of Mid Calder thought that his parishioners in 1839 were kept in such "habits of constant industry as to have little leisure for indulging in the practice of the popular games and amusements which formerly prevailed". If Carse was aware, as surely he must have been, of the careering social changes, then his pictures must be allowed the value of records consciously made before it was too late.

Indeed, Carse was no more than a reporter simply recording the episodes that fell under his eye in the normal course of events. Instead his historical and antiquarian tastes led him to invent pictorial situations, or reconstruct the narratives of poems that would illustrate life as it had been lived in rural Scotland in the recent or even the remote past. He does not seem to have been at all interested in the major events or outstanding figures of history but rather in the customs and changes of ordinary social life. Fig 6 is a case in point. This drawing, which is misleadingly inscribed with the title "Cockellar Sow" (but not in Carse's hand) in fact illustrates a poem *Christ's Kirk on the Green* published and completed with two extra cantos by Allan Ramsay, and supposed to have been composed by James I, the poet king. The poem describes a country dance which turns into a bloodthirsty free fight. The disasters which overtake the principal characters are easily recognisable in Carse's illustration, including the lucky escape of the musician who hides behind the waggon during the fighting. The costumes are a brave if inaccurate attempt at medieval dress, by an artist who can have had no access to authentic sources.

The mysteriously titled *Doonies versus the Croonies on New Year's Day*, (fig 7) which seems to be set on the Lothian or Berwickshire coast, depicts a very old custom, a mass football game traditionally played over much of Scotland in the nineteenth century by the inhabitants of the upper end of a town against those of the lower end. The two sides were normally distinguished by the titles Uppies and Doonies. Carse's nomenclature seems to be a unique variant but, according to John MacQueen of the School of Scottish Studies, the term Croonie is an obvious parallel with the term Uppie, and must mean a person connected with the crown or upper end. The game still continued in parts of the borders until the middle of this century.

Plate 7 shows guisers who have come to perform their ancient midwinter ritual play in a farmhouse kitchen. Two characters in the party have been inscribed by Carse with their traditional names, Judas, who holds the bag, and Sir William Wallace. The play,

like those described in Fraser's *Golden Bough*, was concerned with death and resurrection. Carse's rendering is complicated by the introduction of an episode a little like that later described by Hardy in the mumming episode in *The Return of the Native*. Amongst the guising party (who should all be male) a girl has managed to conceal herself using the guiser's loose gown or smock and elaborate hat. The farmer's son who has just

Fig 8
ANDRO WI' HIS CUTTY GUN, c. 1817.

recognised her, whisks off her hat. A candle is held up to light her feminine features, whilst the farmhouse audience express amusement or astonishment at the discovery. It is not known whether this illustrates any published story, but in the highly finished *Andro wi' his cutty gun* of c.1817, (fig 8) Carse takes an old Scots song,

> "*The gudewife brought the kebbuck ben,*
> *Wi girdle cakes weel toasted brown;*
> *Weel does the canny kimmer ken,*
> *They gar the swats gae glibber down;*"

A kebbuck is a cheese, a canny kimmer, is a cunning old lady. Swats are beer or ale.

The scene is thus set in a single roomed country inn where Andro, the sportsman, is being fed dry oatcakes and cheese to encourage his consumption of liquor. Carse's costumes, which should be compared with the nineteenth-century costumes of *The Arrival of the Country Relations* indicate his desire to set the ballad at some point in the previous century. In particular the girl's waisted dress, tight laced bodice and low frilled neckline, which Carse could have seen in eighteenth century portraits, contrasts with the curious early nineteenth century fashion for a waist elevated to armpit level.

In this picture, and in his illustration (fig 9) Act V Scene II of Ramsay's *Gentle Shepherd* Carse depicts the type of old fashioned hearth used before the built-in chimney flue in the gable wall became standard. Wood is heaped on a free standing iron brazier in the centre of the floor and an iron cooking pot is slung over it on a chain. The smoke may, or may not find its way out through the roof. The rendering of such details, together with the textures and

Fig 9
Illustration to Ramsay's poem
THE GENTLE SHEPHERD, c. 1812.

patterns of old brass pans, pewter measures, painted crockery and wine glasses of antique form, obviously gave Carse the greatest pleasure.

Not all Carse's pictures are comedies. His *Bible Reading at a Cottage Door* (plate 10) and *Grace before Meat* (plate 5) are peaceful

Fig 10
A SHEPHERD IN A SNOWSTORM, 1805.

and grave in their mood, and the illustration to Thomson's poem *Winter* (fig 10) represents a hill shepherd lost, and staggering through the snow drift in which he will shortly perish. The little sketch of *Covenanters in a Thunderstorm* (fig 11) must either be unfinished or is a study for a larger work. It has none of the lavish period detail of some of Carse's other pictures and the mood is sombre, even tragic. Dated 1810 it must be the earliest attempt in Scottish art to depict the tribulations of the Covenanters.

Even the three historical novels in which the covenanting movement was tackled, Scott's *Old Mortality,* Galt's *Ringan Gilhaize,* and Hogg's *Brownie of Bodsbeck* belong a decade later than Carse's picture, and George Harvey's series of Covenanting paintings was not begun until 1830. Carse's relative

Fig 11
COVENANTERS IN A THUNDERSTORM, 1810.

lack of technical sophistication, when compared with the knowledge and fluency of Scott the writer or the sentimental skills of Harvey the painter, should not blind one to the novelty and originality of his choice of subject.

Carse's two most ambitious paintings— apart from his *George IV Landing at Leith*— and his most elaborate attempts to portray old Scottish pastimes, are his *Village Ba' game* and *Penny Wedding,* painted c.1818 and 1819 respectively, while he was living in London. Both are crowd scenes, full of vigorous action. The *Ba' game* echoes the subject matter of Carse's *Doonies and Croonies*. *The Penny Wedding* on the other hand echoes the subject and title of the picture Wilkie was engaged on from 1817 to 1819. It is unlikely that this is merely chance. As a fellow Scot working in London Carse must surely have had easy access to Wilkie's studio and would have known what he was up to. The coincidence of the two *Penny Weddings* is in fact the culmination of a series of paintings on related subjects produced by both men over the previous six years. In 1813 Carse had showed *The Rival Wooers* and *The Chapman* or *Scots Pedlar* at the British Institution. In 1814 Wilkie, at the RA, showed *The Refusal from Burns' song of Duncan Gray* (a wooing scene) and *The Pedlar*. In 1815 Carse at the British Institution exhibited *Duncan Gray,* and *The Chapman* or *Scotch Pedlar.* In 1819 each exhibited his own *Penny Wedding,* Carse at the BI, Wilkie at the Royal Academy. Although both paintings share features which derive from David Allan, and both introduce a new feature—the man who pulls forward his bonnet whilst saying a hasty grace, they are otherwise dissimilar in character. Wilkie's scene is full of nostalgic sentiment, distanced from the viewer in time as well as space, for the costume is that of the late eighteenth century. Looking at Carse's picture the spectator is thrust into a whirl of activity. The centre of the floor is crammed with dancers. To the right seated shepherds or farmers gorge themselves on a ham. Behind them the hat for voluntary contributions—guests at a Penny Wedding paid their share—is passed to a pair of men who seem indignantly declaring that they have paid already. To the left the newly wedded pair are offered glasses of punch, and congratulated. The wrist and hand of the bride, charming in her pink shawl, are held by her elderly father, whilst both her parents gaze fondly at the young couple. In the facial expressions, as in the details of the old lady's sprigged shawl, the young man's folded stock, the glasses, punch bowl and willow pattern jug on the table, this is one of Carse's happiest efforts.

PLATES

1. Willow Cathedral.
Watercolour heightened with bodycolour, 20.5 × 25.5.

2. Drawing Room at Midfield Cottage, 1803.
Oil on panel, 45.7 × 64.8.

3. Arrival of the Country Relations, 1812.
Oil on canvas, 52.1 × 69.8.

4. Sportsman Refreshing himself at an Inn.
Oil on canvas, 62.2 × 73.7.

5. Grace before Meat.
Oil on canvas, 41.9 × 52.1.

6. Scene from the Gentle Shepherd, c. 1812.
Oil on panel, 38.7 × 31.1.

7. The Guisers.
Pen and ink and wash on grey paper, 32.3 × 52.6.

8. The Penny Wedding, c. 1819.
Oil on panel, 88.2 × 131.5.

9. The Village Ba' Game, 1818.
Oil on canvas, 88.9 × 132.2.

10. Bible Reading at a Cottage Door.
Watercolour on cream paper, 42.0 × 34.8.

11. The Country Preacher.
Watercolour, 47.0 × 63.9.

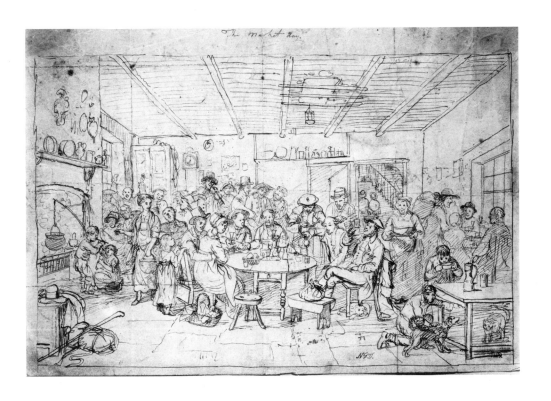

12. The Market Day.
Pen and ink with red chalk on cream paper, 23.0 × 33.7.

ALEXANDER CARSE BIBLIOGRAPHY

Printed Sources

ROBERT BRYDALL
Art in Scotland Edinburgh and London 1879,
pps. 267-8.

W. D. MACKAY
The Scottish School of Painting London 1906,
p. 141.

JAMES L. CAW
Scottish Painting Past and Present Edinburgh
1908, p. 106.

DAVID & FRANCINA IRWIN
Scottish Painters at Home and Abroad London
1975, pps. 190-1.

NATIONAL GALLERY OF
SCOTLAND
Bulletin Number I 1975.

Manuscripts in the Scottish Records Office

Letter to the Trustees of the Spalding Fund
NG1/59/117 and NG1/59/13 (to Royal
Institution).

NG1/59/116 Meeting of Spalding Trustees
21st February 1843 includes an order to pay
Carse his annuity,

NG1/59/117 includes a letter from John
Brooks 13 September 1843 mentioning
"The late Mr A. Carse".

CHECKLIST OF PAINTINGS AND DRAWINGS BY ALEXANDER CARSE

(This is not a complete list but includes the more important
of his works still known to be extant.)

Measurements are in centimetres height before width.

OIL PAINTINGS

[1.] DRAWING ROOM OF
MIDFIELD COTTAGE,
LASSWADE
Oil on panel. 45.7 × 64.8
Inscribed on the reverse: *Alex
Carse 1803/Drawing room in
Midfield Cottage with Lady
Molesworth, Miss Brown & Mr and
Mrs Campbell.*
Private collection.

[2.] GARDEN FRONT OF
MIDFIELD COTTAGE,
LASSWADE
Oil on panel. 43.2 × 58.1
Inscribed on the reverse: *Alex
Carse 1807/Midfield Cottage* (part
of the label missing).
Private collection.

[3.] ENTRANCE FRONT OF
MIDFIELD COTTAGE,
LASSWADE
Oil on panel. 43.2 × 58.1
Inscribed on the reverse: *Alex
Carse 1807/Midfield cottage with Mr
and Mrs Campbell, Mrs James
Hamilton and Duncan McTavish.*
Private collection.

[4.] A SHEPHERD IN A
SNOWSTORM
Oil on canvas. 41.3 × 33.7
An illustration to Thomson's
poem *Winter*.
Private collection.

[5.] COVENANTERS IN A
THUNDERSTORM
*Oil on paper mounted on
canvas. 41.9 × 36.8*
Inscribed on the reverse:
*Covenanters in a thunderstorm—a
sketch by Al* Carse Aug 17 1810*.
Richard and Vanessa Emerson
collection.

[6.] THE PEDLAR'S VISIT
Oil on panel. 38.7 × 31.1
J. D. M. Robertson collection.

[7.] SCENE FROM 'THE
GENTLE SHEPHERD'
Oil on panel. 38.7 × 31.1
Carse exhibited two paintings
from this poem in 1812.
J. D. M. Robertson collection.

[8.] SCENE FROM 'THE
GENTLE SHEPHERD'
Oil on panel. 38.7 × 31.1
Private collection.

[9.] ARRIVAL OF THE
COUNTRY RELATIONS
Oil on canvas. 52.1 × 69.8
First exhibited 1812.
The Duke of Buccleuch and
Queensberry, KT collection.

[10.] LANDSCAPE WITH
PEASANTS
Oil on canvas. 62.2 × 74.9
The Duke of Buccleuch and
Queensberry, KT collection.

[11.] THE NEW WEB
Oil on canvas. 47.3 × 62.5
First exhibited 1813.
National Gallery of Scotland.

[12.] GRACE BEFORE MEAT
Oil on canvas. 41.9 × 52.1
Private collection.

[13.] SPORTSMAN
REFRESHING HIMSELF AT
AN INN
Oil on canvas. 62.2 × 73.7
Private collection.

[14.] ANDRO WI' HIS CUTTY
GUN
Oil on canvas. 66 × 86.4
Traditionally dated 1817.
Private collection.

[15.] THE DOONIES
VERSUS THE CROONIES ON
NEW YEAR'S DAY
Oil on canvas. 69.8 × 89.5
J. D. M. Robertson collection.

[16.] THE VILLAGE BA'
GAME
Oil on canvas. 88.9 × 132.2
Signed and dated: *A. Carse/1818.*
Dundee Museums and Art
Galleries.

[17.] THE PENNY WEDDING
Oil on panel. 88.2 × 131.5
Flight Lieutenant G. N. Statham
collection.

[18.] BRAWL OUTSIDE AN
ALE HOUSE
Oil on canvas. 43.2 × 53.4
Signed and dated: *A. Carse 1822.*
National Gallery of Scotland.

[19.] GEORGE IV LANDING
AT LEITH IN 1822
Oil on canvas. 160.1 × 362.0
The City of Edinburgh Museums
and Art Galleries.

WATERCOLOURS
AND DRAWINGS

[20.] LEITH RACES
*Pen and ink and colour wash on cream
paper. 43.8 × 59.5*
Signed and dated: *AC 1794.*
Private collection.

[21.] THE RETURN FROM
LEITH RACES
*Pen and ink and colour wash on cream
paper. 45.6 × 60.0*
Signed and dated twice: *AC 1794.*
Edinburgh City Libraries.

[22.] OLDHAMSTOCKS FAIR
*Pen and ink and watercolour on light
buff paper. 39.5 × 63.1*
Signed and dated: *Alex* Carse
1796.*
National Gallery of Scotland.

[23.] OLDHAMSTOCKS FAIR
Watercolour. 46.4 × 63.5
Glasgow Art Gallery and
Museum.

[24.] CHRIST'S KIRK ON THE
GREEN
*Pen and ink and colour wash on cream
paper. 29.5 × 44.5*
Inscribed below in pencil (but not
in Carse's own hand): *Cockellar
Sow/A Carse Fecit.*
An illustration of the poem
Christ's Kirk on the Green
attributed to James I.
National Gallery of Scotland.

[25.] MELVILLE PAPER MILL
Gouache. 33.0 × 46.7
Dated 1797.
F. C. B. Richards, Esq. collection.

[26.) BROOMHOUSE PAPER
MILL
Gouache. 33.0 × 47.0
Signed and dated: *A Carse 1797.*
Private collection.

[27.] WILLOW CATHEDRAL
*Watercolour heightened with
bodycolour. 20.5 × 25.5*
Drawn for Sir James Hall of
Dunglass c1794–7 to illustrate Sir
James' theory that Gothic
architecture derived from earlier
buildings of wattle. The Willow
Cathedral had been woven for Sir
James by a country craftsman.
British Architectural Library/
RIBA collection.

[28.] SOUTH VIEW OF LEITH
*Pen and ink and colour wash on cream
paper.   46.6 × 62.3*
Signed and inscribed below: *A
Carse Delin^t/South View of Leith.*
National Gallery of Scotland.

[29.] EDINBURGH FROM ST
ANTHONY'S CHAPEL
*Pen and black ink and wash on cream
paper.*
Inscribed twice in ink top left, and
in pencil on the verso: *Edinburgh
from St Anthony's Chapel/Original
drawing in Indian ink by /A Carse
1799.* Inscribed in ink on the
verso: *Edin 1799 by A Carse.*
National Gallery of Scotland.

[30.] A SHEPHERD IN A
SNOWSTORM
*Watercolour heightened with white on
paper.   42.5 × 33.9*
Signed and dated twice:
A Carse 1805.
An illustration to Thomson's
poem *Winter.*
The Syndics of the Fitzwilliam
Museum, Cambridge.

[31.] THE JOLLY BEGGARS
*Pen and brown ink and wash on cream
paper.   19.0 × 24.8*
An illustration to the poem by
Robert Burns.
National Gallery of Scotland.

[32.] TAM O'SHANTER
WATCHING CUTTY SARK
DANCE WITH THE WITCHES
IN KIRK ALLOWAY
*Pencil and coloured wash on cream
paper.   23.0 × 30.4*
Inscribed on a tombstone left: *Hic
jacet/A Carse.*
An illustration to Robert Burns'
poem *Tam O'Shanter.*
National Gallery of Scotland.

[33.] THE COTTER'S
SATURDAY NIGHT
*Pen and ink on cream paper.
26.7 × 36.0*
An illustration to the poem by
Robert Burns.
National Gallery of Scotland.

[34.] THE WITCHES' LATE-
WAKE
*Pencil with coloured wash and body
colour on cream paper.   19.1 × 25.0*
A late, or more correctly lyke
wake, was the ceremony of
watching a corpse the night before
the funeral. In 1815 Carse
exhibited a painting of this title
illustrating a poem by William
Carse.
National Gallery of Scotland.

[35.] THE MARKET DAY
*Pen and ink with red chalk on cream
paper.   23.0 × 33.7*
Inscribed in ink top: *The Market
Day.*
National Gallery of Scotland.

[36.] THE COUNTRY
PREACHER
Watercolour.   47.0 × 63.9
Glasgow Art Gallery and
Museum.

[37.] THE GUISERS
*Pen and ink and wash on grey paper.
32.3 × 52.6*
The figure holding the bag, far
left, is inscribed: *Judas.* The figure
to the right of the fiddler is
inscribed: *Sir Wm Wallace.*
National Gallery of Scotland.

[38.] A MAN SMOKING A
PIPE
*Black chalk heightened with white on
grey paper.   32.2 × 26.0*
Signed in pencil (but not in Carse's
hand).
A study for the figure of Andro in
Carse's painting illustrating the
ballad *Andro wi' his cutty gun*
(Private collection).
National Gallery of Scotland.

[39.] BIBLE READING AT A
COTTAGE DOOR
*Watercolour on cream paper.
42.0 × 34.8*
National Gallery of Scotland.